American Cars
of the 1930s

edited by Bart H. Vanderveen

ISBN 0 85429 543 7

A **FOULIS** Motoring Book

First published, in the Auto Library series, by Frederick Warne, 1971
Reprinted 1973, 1975, 1977, 1981, 1985

© Olyslager Organisation BV 1971

Published by:
Haynes Publishing Group
Sparkford, Nr. Yeovil,
Somerset BA22 7JJ

Haynes Publications Inc,
861 Lawrence Drive, Newbury Park,
California 91320 USA

Other titles in this series

The Jeep
Cross-Country Cars from 1945
Half-Tracks
Tanks and Transport Vehicles of World War 2
Armour on Wheels to 1942
Fire-Fighting Vehicles 1840–1950
Fire and Crash Vehicles from 1950
Trucks of the Sixties and Seventies
Wreckers and Recovery Vehicles
Passenger Vehicles 1893–1940
Buses and Coaches from 1940
Fairground and Circus Transport

American Cars of the 1930s
American Cars of the 1940s

American Cars of the 1950s
American Cars of the 1960s
American Cars of the 1970s

American Trucks of the Early Thirties
American Trucks of the Late Thirties

British Cars of the Early Thirties
British Cars of the Late Thirties
British Cars of the Early Forties
British Cars of the Late Forties
British Cars of the Early Fifties
British Cars of the Late Fifties
British Cars of the Early Sixties

Motorcycles to 1945
Motorcycles from 1945

This 'picture album' deals with American cars of the period 1930 to 1939. The emphasis is on the popular models of the 'Big Three', namely General Motors, Ford and Chrysler, and the largest 'independents' such as Hudson, Nash, Packard and Studebaker, rather than the more glamorous 'classics' such as Cord, Duesenberg, Marmon and Pierce Arrow. The intention is firstly to present a review of this important decade of American automotive production, during which time square box-shaped body styles gave way to streamlined notch- and fast-back styling, and secondly to provide a handy reference work which serves as a means of identifying the various cars by make and model year.

Many of these 'American' cars were actually produced outside the United States, for a variety of reasons. Several popular types were assembled or manufactured (or partly manufactured) in Canada, where assembly and manufacturing plants had been set up, mainly in Ontario, because it was reasonably close to Detroit. In addition to supplying home-market customers, these Canadian products were marketed in Britain and throughout the Commonwealth. Export to these countries was usually in CKD (completely knocked down) or PKD (partly knocked down) form, final assembly and again part-manufacturing usually taking place in the country of destination. In the process there was plenty of opportunity to 'tailor' certain types of cars for a particular market, not only by fitting, for example, small-bore engines in order to meet (or bend!) local horsepower taxation regulations but also by changing marque names. For example: the Plymouth, Chrysler's cheapest range of cars, was marketed in Britain under the Chrysler name, which was the Chrysler Corporation's top-line marque. This process became popularly known as 'badge engineering' and still takes place. Sometimes of course this is done because a certain marque may already have been registered by another manufacturer. Many cars and CKD packs were also exported direct from the United States to distributors and assembly plants in various countries in Europe, Asia, Africa, South America etc.

An important point to remember when reviewing American cars (whether of US or Canadian origin) is that 'model years' are different from 'calendar years' and as such were not always strictly adhered to by distributors in overseas markets. If, for example, in a certain export market a surplus of a certain type of American car occurred at the end of the 'model year' (often as early as August-September) the distributor would continue selling it, even into the next calendar year, with the result that it would be registered in the year following its 'model year'. Invariably such left-over stock of the previous year's models would be sold at attractive 'clearance' prices.

American autos of the nineteen thirties were extremely popular all over the world and their ruggedness, combined with powerful engines, spacious bodies and competitive prices, made them particularly attractive in many overseas countries where large-scale motorisation was still in its infancy. Henry Ford's 'Tin Lizzy' Model T had of course been instrumental in creating much goodwill for American cars and his success-ive A, B and V8 models could be found in the most distant corners of the globe. The enormous competition from General Motors, Chrysler and the rest proved to be of great benefit to potential buyers.

The following pages have been laid out on a year-by-year basis and, as far as possible, each make appears in alphabetical order under the section relating to its particular year for easy reference. Obviously the book is not a complete survey but it is thought to be sufficiently comprehensive to meet the need for a work of this kind. The models included could be divided into three categories, namely USA domestic production (with standard or custom bodywork), models assembled/produced in other countries, and exported chassis with 'foreign' bodywork. As a result there are probably some 'American' car types which may never have 'set tyre' on American soil.

Piet Olyslager MSIA, MSAE, KIVI

1930

During 1930 the American automotive industry produced 2,784,745 passenger cars and 571,241 trucks and buses. This figure (about twice the number of vehicles taxed in Great Britain) compared very unfavourably with 1929 which had shown figures of 4,587,400 and 771,020 respectively The reason was that America as well as much of the rest of the world lay deep in an economic crisis. The Wall Street crash of the previous year had caused a slump which also affected Europe and the British Commonwealth and meant, or was going to mean, the end of many a car manufacturer. Other US statistics for 1930 (the 1929 figures are given in brackets) show that there were some 341,000 (471,000) automobile workers and 48,658 (52,588) motor vehicle dealers. The wholesale value of cars, trucks and buses produced amounted to $2,035 (3,413) million. The total number of US vehicle registrations was 26,545,000 (26,501,000) of which slightly under 3·5 (3·4) million were trucks and buses. On the technical side, most 1930 US cars had flat-base wheels with tyre sizes varying from 20 to 18 in. and double-bar bumpers, usually with a rounded profile. Mechanical fuel pumps had begun to replace the vacuum tank type fuel feed system.

4A: **Buick Six,** built in Canada (McLaughlin). Last year of six-cylinder Buicks. Three Series: 40, 50 and 60.
4B: **Cadillac Series 353 V8** Cabriolet Imperial by Fleetwood. V12 models and hydraulic valve lifters made their appearance.
4C: **Chevrolet Universal Series AD** Coach. 'Stovebolt Six' ohv engine had replaced four-cylinder for 1929 model year. Body by Fisher.
4D: **Chrysler 77 Six** had 4340-cc 93-bhp engine. Shown here is Canadian-built rhd export model with 27·3 HP (RAC) rating.

4A Buick

4D Chrysler

4C Chevrolet

4B Cadillac

5A Cord

5A: **Cord L29** bristled with unconventional design and engineering features such as front-wheel drive and double ¼-elliptic springs.

5B: **Cord L29 Brougham** was first introduced in 1929 and was powered by eight-cylinder 125-bhp Lycoming engine. Continued until 1932.

5C: **DeSoto CK Six.** This make was introduced by Chrysler in 1928 to fill the gap between Plymouth and Dodge.

5D: **Dodge DD Six** Sedan, powered by 189·8-cu in. L-head engine with 5·2:1 compression ratio developing 60 bhp at 3400 rpm.

5E: **Dodge DC Eight** Coupé. This was Dodge Brothers' first eight-cylinder. Output was 75 bhp, cubic capacity 220·7 cu in.

5B Cord

5D Dodge

5C DeSoto

5E Dodge

6A: The Dynamic New **Erskine** Club Sedan, one of a low-price range of models by Studebaker.

6B: **Essex Super Six Challenger** Phaeton as marketed in Great Britain by Hudson Essex Motors Ltd of Chiswick, W.4, at £245. Engine was 2638-cc L-head of 18·2 HP (RAC). Essex was lower-price model range of Hudson Motor Co.

6C: **Ford Model A** had $103\frac{1}{2}$-in. wb and in the US there were sixteen body styles. This Convertible Coupé model has survived in England. Roadster version looked rather similar but had folding windshield (screen).

6D: **Ford Model A** Special Convertible coachwork by Schutter & van Bakel of Amsterdam, Netherlands. 35 of these were produced in 1930–31 for Amsterdam Ford dealer. Nearly 4·5 million Model As were produced from late 1927 until early 1932.

6C Ford

6A Erskine

6B Essex

6D Ford

7A: Hudson Great Eight Roadster on short-wheelbase chassis. One of ten body styles on two chassis lengths (wb 119 and 126 in.). Windshield could be opened, or folded flat completely.

7B: Hudson Great Eight. Front view of Roadster. Double-bar front bumper was typical of 1929—31 American cars. Note large headlamps. Colours: 'cheerfully smart, or subdued and dignified, as you prefer'.

7C: Hudson Great Eight Brougham on long-wheelbase chassis. Fabric-covered rear-quarter panels and 'Landau Arms'. Wire wheels and two spares were optional. (Standard: wood wheels, one spare rim, five tyres).

7D: LaSalle Series 340 V8 Seven-passenger Sedan. LaSalle was introduced by Cadillac in 1927 to enter the medium-price market. 1930 models had 90-bhp V8 engine. Coachwork by Fisher.

7A Hudson

7C Hudson

7B Hudson

7D LaSalle

8A: Lincoln V8. Period advertisement (July 1930) showing Barker Pullman Limousine DeVille, one of many special body styles available on this top-line chassis of the Ford Motor Co.
8B: Marquette Series 30 was Buick's cheapest range. There were six models, all with 114-in. wb, ranging from Business Coupé (Model 36) at $990 to four-door Sedan (Model 37) at $1060.
8C: Nash Eight. In 1930 Nash Motors introduced an eight-cylinder engine. Sedan shown was converted for running on paraffin in Holland when petrol was rationed (c. 1946).
8D: Oldsmobile F30 Six Sedan, shown here with disc wheels, priced just under $1000 in 1929/30. Oldsmobile also offered a smart but short-lived luxury V8 model named Viking.

LUXURIOUS PERFORMANCE

DIGNITY AND BEAUTY

It is hard to say what most delights that ever-growing number of Lincoln owners throughout the world ↛ ↛ Is it the knowledge that in no other product such strict creative standards are observed? ↛ ↛ Is it the feeling of pride that so many gallant craftsmen achieve here a new and unheard-of excellence? ↛ ↛ Is it enjoyment of Lincoln's timeless style that never grows old? ↛ ↛ Is it the thrill that comes from Lincoln's complete mastery of all gradients and all distances? ↛ ↛ Or, do Lincoln owners enjoy most the sense of luxury fulfilment that goes even beyond bodily comfort, that attains complete mental confidence and assurance? ↛ ↛ This much is known. The combination of all that is Lincoln, the endless variety of Lincoln enjoyments put together, brings a completely new motoring consciousness to Lincoln owners and passengers ↛ ↛ See Lincoln body styles built by Lincoln's own craftsmen — also creations by the leading coachbuilders of the world, designed to dwell in distinguished harmony with this, as fine a motor car as it is possible to produce. Lincoln Division, Ford Motor Company Limited, 88 Regent Street, London, W.1 ↛ ↛

THE LINCOLN

8A Lincoln

8C Nash

8B Marquette

8D Oldsmobile

9A: Packard DeLuxe Eight, Seventh Series, Model 745. Special Dutch coachwork by Schutter & van Bakel of Amsterdam. Spotlight at front was manually operated from driver's seat. Note disc wheels and large luggage compartment at rear. Also known as 'Big Eight'. Engine had $3\frac{1}{2} \times 5$ in. bore and stroke and developed 106 bhp. Wheelbase $145\frac{1}{2}$ in. Companion model was Custom Eight (wb $140\frac{1}{2}$ in.); both were in production for one year from August 1929.

9B: Packard Standard Eight, Seventh Series, Model 733 Phaeton. One of ten body styles available on this $134\frac{1}{2}$-in. wb chassis, which was in production from 20 August 1929 until 14 August 1930. Prices varied from $2425 for 401 Phaeton and 402 Roadster to to $2775 for 405 Limousine. A companion model on $127\frac{1}{2}$-in. wb chassis was the Model 726 which, however, was only available with one body style (403 Sedan, $2375). Prices shown are those at time of introduction.

9A Packard

9B Packard

10A Plymouth

10A: Plymouth 30U Four Convertible Coupé with dickey seat. It was Chrysler Corporation's low-price make, introduced in 1928. In spite of the stock market crash of 1929, Plymouth sales in the USA boomed, especially when in 1930 all Chrysler, DeSoto and Dodge dealers were given Plymouth franchises.
Until 1933 all Plymouth cars had L-head Four engines; in 1930 this was a 196·1 cu in. unit, developing 48 bhp at 2800 rpm. Wheelbase was 109 in.

10B: Pontiac 6-30B Six Sedan sold at $825 and differed from 1929 model mainly by way of a new slanting windshield and improved brakes. Originally a companion car to the Oakland, the more popular Pontiac soon went ahead of Oakland and in 1931 the latter was discontinued.
10C: Studebaker President Eight State Sedan was seven-seater with 135-in. wb. Six wire-spoke wheels and luggage grid were standard equipment.

10B Pontiac

10C Studebaker

11A Auburn

This was another bad sales year for the American motor industry and model changes were minimal. Due to the nationwide economic illness, following the Great Depression, sales of cars and trucks took another dive to 1,973,090 and 416,648 respectively. During the year the 50 millionth US motor vehicle was produced, but at the year's end the number of motor vehicle dealers had dwindled to under 44,000 (there were 52,588 in 1929) and the total number of vehicle registrations had dropped to 2,390,000. Many manufacturers had available large and luxurious models of the type the public had indicated it wanted until the Great Depression came, and these powerful cars were now offered at reduced prices. Many manufacturers introduced refinements such as free-wheeling (available on some 15 makes) and synchromesh transmissions. Hydraulic brakes were still reserved for the more expensive cars. Among the few new makes introduced in 1931 were Studebaker's Rockne and the DeVaux. Both were short-lived. The latter was launched in January in Grand Rapids, Michigan, and looked quite promising. However, after 14 months the company got into financial difficulty and was taken over by Continental, the engine makers, who continued it under their own name (models: Beacon, Flyer, Red Seal) until 1934.

11A: **Auburn 898 Eight.** There were two basic models, the Standard 898 and the 898A Custom series, each with seven body styles.
11B: **Buick Eight Series 50.** Cheapest Sedan in Buick's 1931 range was this Model 50 two-door ($1035); costliest was 90L ($2035).
11C: **Cadillac Series 452A V16** Transformable Town Brougham by Fleetwood. Wheelbase 148 in. List price of a typical Cadillac V16: $5950. The company also offered V8 and V12 models.

11B Buick

11C Cadillac

12A Chevrolet

12B Chevrolet

Chevrolet Independence Series AE

Mechanically, the 1931 Chevrolets were not much different from the 1930 models but wb was 2 in. longer (109 in.) and most of the bodywork was restyled. There were 14 models using this chassis and in addition a Sedan Delivery (van) and three commercial chassis options. The straight black-enamel headlamp tiebar was replaced by a curved chrome-plated one and there were more louvres in the hood (bonnet). Shown here are:

12A: Convertible Cabriolet. This car has survived in Czechoslovakia and is in regular use.

12B: Right-hand drive Phaeton, surviving in England. Note folding windshield.

12C: Special Town Sedan with open front compartment and Roadster windshield.

12D: Three-window Coupé DeLuxe with grille in front of radiator shell.

12C Chevrolet

12D Chevrolet

13A: **Chrysler Imperial Custom Eight** was new in 1931 and superbly elegant. It had a 384-cu in. engine, developing 125 bhp. The chassis was used by various makers of luxury coachwork.

13B: **DeSoto SA Six** had 109⅜-in. wb and 205·3-cu in. engine. Also available was the 114-in. wb Model CF Eight, distinguishable by two-tier bumpers. Power output was 72 and 77 bhp respectively.

13C: **Dodge Brothers** period advertisement. The Company had been founded by John and Horace Dodge in 1914 and became part of the Chrysler Corporation in 1928. The word 'dependability' was first used by Dodge.

13A Chrysler

13B DeSoto

DODGE DEPENDABILITY

NEW DODGE SIX SEDAN $845

New Beauty AND THE DEPENDABILITY FOR WHICH DODGE IS FAMED

You naturally expect that Dodge, having earned a world-wide reputation for dependability, should prize that reputation. And Dodge does prize it. » » The beautiful New Dodge Six and Eight are exactly the kind of car you would expect Dodge to build. » » With all of their new smartness and luxury, they hold fast to every Dodge principle of excellence. They carry still higher a fine tradition for cars of long life, out-standing economy and dependability. » » The New Dodge Six and Eight are larger, finer, faster, smoother and more comfortable. Yet they remain at traditional Dodge price-levels. » » Today, more than ever before, it is important to buy a car that will cost little to run during a long period of life. And never before have Dodge cars embodied so much that guarantees satisfaction and economy through years of service.

Carrying on a Fine Tradition: LONGER WHEELBASES give gracious riding comfort and smart, fleet appearance—DOUBLE-DROP FRAME, box-type, providing low-swung grace and great strength of chassis—ADVANCED PERFORMANCE from engines of larger size and greater efficiency—MONO-PIECE STEEL BODIES, insulated, jointless and squeakless, extremely strong, with Bedford Cord upholstery and other fine appointments—INTERNAL HYDRAULIC BRAKES, safe, weatherproof, positive, self-equalizing—WIRE WHEELS, five wire wheels at no extra cost.

© 1931 by Dodge Brothers Corporation

New Dodge Six $815 to $845, New Dodge Eight $1095 to $1135, Standard Six $735 to $835, Standard Eight $995 to $1095. F.O.B. Factory.

13C Dodge

14A: **Essex Super Six Challenger** Sedan was quite popular in Great Britain where it sold at £225. Engine was 2368-cc L-head, rated at 18·2 HP (RAC). Wire wheels were optional extra.

14B: **Ford Model A** Coupé (Type 45B) was one of 18 body styles available. In Britain there was also the Model AF which had reduced-bore 2-litre 14·9 HP (treasury rating) engine.

14C: **Ford Model A** Panel Delivery DeLuxe (Type 130B) was based on the 103½-in. wb car chassis and was, one of over 60 commercial and truck models offered in the 1931 catalogue.

14D: **Ford Model A** Phaeton (Type 35B), used by the (British) Indian army as a staff car. In April 1931 the 20 millionth Ford was produced and a V8 engine was under way.

14A Essex

14B Ford

14C Ford

14D Ford

15A: **Hudson Great Eight** seven-passenger Sedan. This luxurious model was built on a 126-in. wb and featured adjustable front and rear seats (which could also be cranked vertically) and hydraulic shock absorbers which could be controlled for ride comfort from the driver's seat. Engine cubic capacity was $3\frac{1}{2}$ litres.

15B: **LaSalle V8** Convertible Coupé on Series 345A chassis. Engine produced 95 bhp at 3400 rpm. LaSalle cars were produced by Cadillac from 1927 until 1940 and were 'lower-priced carbon copies of the Caddy'. Model shown had 134-in. wb, resulting in long 'rear deck'. Prices started at about $2295.

15C: **Lincoln V8** Sport Phaeton, one of various types available. In addition to factory-built bodies this high-grade chassis was available with the work of well-known coachbuilders such as Dietrich and Waterhouse. Lincoln was founded in 1920 and became a division of the Ford Motor Co. in 1922. Model shown had 145-in. wb and 120-bhp engine.

15B LaSalle

15A Hudson

15C Lincoln

16A: **Nash 870** Sedan was one of 24 models offered in 1931 by this once-famous manufacturer. Only five of these had a six-cylinder engine, the others being Eights. The Eight-70 had 116-in. wb and this Sedan was priced at $995. Specimen shown has been preserved in the Netherlands.

16B: **Oldsmobile F31 Six** Sedan. 1931 Oldsmobiles had synchromesh gearbox and downdraught carburettor for the first time. Note light-coloured spokes of wood wheels. Fisher bodywork was similar to that used for other General Motors products—Chevrolet and Pontiac. Oldsmobile was founded as early as 1896 and taken over by General Motors in 1909.

16C: **Packard Standard Eight, Ninth Series, Model 901** Sedan. This five-seater had a 129½-in. wb and carried body style number 503. The Model 901 (Sedan only) and its 136½-in. wb companion Model 902 series (12 body styles) were in production from June 1931 until January 1933. Engine developed 110 bhp.

16A Nash

16B Oldsmobile

16C Packard

17A: **Plymouth PA Four** Coupé had $109\frac{3}{8}$-in. wb and 196-cu in. engine developing 56 bhp. Sales of Plymouth cars soared to 109,487 during this generally bad Depression year in which several car manufacturers went bankrupt. There were also two- and four-door Sedan, Business Coupé and Roadster, Roadster with Dickey, and Convertible Phaeton body styles.

17B: **Pontiac 401 Six** looked much like contemporary Chevrolet, except for radiator grille. Engine was L-head with $3\frac{5}{16} \times 3\frac{7}{8}$ in. bore and stroke (200 cu in.). Complete model range consisted of three Coupés (Standard, Sport and Convertible) and three Sedans (two-door as shown, Standard four-door and Custom). Wheelbase 112 in. Oakland range similar but 251-cu in. V8 engine (B x S $3\frac{7}{16} \times 3\frac{3}{8}$ in.) and 117-in. wb.

17C: **Reo 8-35 Custom Royale Eight** Coupé. This 5·9-litre car was a luxury companion car to the well-known Flying Cloud. It was styled by Count Alexis de Sakhnoffsky and featured automatic chassis lubrication. Reo derived its name from the initials of Ransom Eli Olds, who had founded Oldsmobile in 1896 and who left in 1904 to start the Reo Motor Car Co.

17B Pontiac

17A Plymouth

17C Reo

1932 opened in the gloomy economic climate of a deepening depression. With the market now 'deader than a doornail' this promised to be the worst year since 1918. Total US production was 1,135,491 cars and 235,187 trucks, a drop of over one million compared with the previous year. Many manufacturers saw their production cut by about half, yet one or two others were not doing too badly. Miraculously, Plymouth production and sales actually increased. Chrysler could claim that its Plymouth was the only car in the industry whose sales rose in 1932 (124,777 vs 109,487). Styling-wise, 1932 was an interesting year with more curves, single bumper bars and drop-centre wheels. Full-skirted fenders made their first appearance (on the Graham), and free-wheels and vacuum-actuated clutches were fashionable. Inside sun visors replaced the familiar exterior shades for improved looks and reduced wind resistance. Production of carburettors, now increasingly of the downdraft type, was more and more monopolised by a few mass-producers; the smaller manufacturers were on the way out. Biggest automotive news of the year was undoubtedly Ford's introduction of a new model with V8 engine, replacing the popular four-cylinder Model A.

18A: **Buick Eight 90** with Cabriolet Coupé coachwork by Vanden Plas of Brussels, Belgium. The Series 90 had a 134-in. wb.
18B: **Buick Eight** Convertible Phaeton, factory-built bodywork available on Series 50, 60 and 90 chassis (wb 114¾, 118 and 134 in. respectively).
18C: **Cadillac Series 355B V8** Town Sedan. Features offered included full-range ride regulator (suspension adjustment control). Also V12 and V16 models.
18D: **Chevrolet Confederate Series BA** DeLuxe Sport Roadster. First Chevrolet with built-in radiator grille. DeLuxe had chromed doors in hood.

18A Buick

18B Buick

18C Cadillac

18D Chevrolet

19A: Chrysler CG Imperial Custom Eight chassis was long (wb 145 in.) and majestic. It was used by various craftsmen/coachbuilders. This double-cowl Phaeton (design LeBaron) was built by Briggs.

19B: DeSoto SC Six Convertible. Along with the other Chrysler Corporation cars the 1932 DeSotos had 'Floating Power' rubber engine mountings and optional free-wheel behind gearbox.

19C: Dodge DM Four Sedan. For the first time since 1928 there was a Dodge Four again. The L-head engine had 92·1×120·7 mm bore and stroke, and developed 65 bhp. Also available were a Roadster, a Phaeton and a two-door Convertible Sedan.

19D: Dodge DK Eight Sedan. 1932 saw introduction of Dodge 'Ram' trademark as radiator cap ornament. DL Six also available.

19A Chrysler

19C Dodge

19B DeSoto

19D Dodge

1932

Ford Model 18 V8 was introduced 9th March 1932, following nearly 4,500,000 Model As. Four-cylinder engine remained available in virtually the same auto, designated **Model B.** The V8, which produced 65 bhp at 3400 rpm, could be seen as Ford's answer to Chevrolet's Six and was an instant success. There were 14 body styles (not counting the B commercials), some of which are shown here:

20A: British Model B Fordor 24 HP was also available as BF Fourteen-Nine (14·9 HP). Resembled Model 18 except for V8 ornaments. Built until 1935.

20B: Model 18 Cabriolet (Type 68). Note V8 ornaments on wheel hub caps and headlamp tiebar. Wheelbase 106 in.

20C: Model 18 Cabriolet with top down and dickey (or rumble) seat opened up. Speed up to 75 mph.

20D: Model B Standard Coupé (Type 45) with 50-bhp four-cylinder engine. V8 engine and dickey seat optional.

20A Ford

20C Ford

20B Ford

20D Ford

21A: **Hudson's Essex Terraplane** replaced earlier Essex range in July. Famous woman pilot Amelia Earhart came to Hudson Motor Car Co. for its christening. Prices started at a low $425.

21B: **Hudson Special.** Six of these vehicles were built for the Japanese Government for military use in Manchuria. Only the rearmost wheels were driven. The spares were idler/support wheels.

21C: **LaSalle Series 345B V8** Victoria Coupé. Body by Fisher. Wheelbase was 136 in. Due to the Depression, Cadillac and LaSalle sales dropped to 8,085 from 29,781 in 1931.

21D: **Lincoln KB V12** was new in 1932 when V8 was discontinued. 145-in. wb chassis was used for a variety of special bodies. Next Lincoln V8s were 9EL and 9EH Cosmopolitan in 1949.

21A Hudson

21C LaSalle

21B Hudson

21D Lincoln

22A: **Marmon V16** Convertible Sedan. The 9·1-litre engine was designed by Colonel Howard Marmon and incorporated wide use of aluminium alloy. It was first introduced in 1931 at $4925 for the complete car. British prices: chassis £1,295, complete £1,625.

22B: **Nash Standard Eight 1070** Sedan. This 121-in. wb model was one of the 1932 2nd Series, introduced in mid-year. Other models in this Series were the Big Six (116-in. wb), Special Eight (128-in.), Advanced Eight (133-in.) and Ambassador Eight (142-in.).

22C: **Oldsmobile L32 Eight** was new for 1932 and resembled the F32 Six in appearance. Shown is the Coach (two-door Sedan) with standard Fisher bodywork. Spare wheel mounting was either at rear, as shown, or in fender well.

22B Nash

22A Marmon

22C Oldsmobile

23A: **Packard Eight DeLuxe, Ninth Series, Model 904** Coupé by Dietrich, formally known as 'Individual Custom Stationary Coupé', Body Model No. 2068. Ninth Series was produced from June 1931 to January 1933.

23B: **Pierce-Arrow Eight** Sedan with characteristic streamlined headlamps. Company was under control of Studebaker and built

eight- and twelve-cylinder models. The V-12 came in $5\frac{1}{2}$- and 7-litre forms, developing up to 175 bhp.

23C: **Pontiac 402 Six** Coach. For 1932 the Oakland was dropped and the Pontiac came as either a Six or Eight. Wheelbase was 114 and 117 in. respectively. Six body styles.

23A Packard

23B Pierce-Arrow

23C Pontiac

24A: **Rockne Six 65** Coupé was produced by Studebaker through its subsidiary the Rockne Motor Corporation which in 1931 was formed to sell low-price cars. Rockne sold relatively well (better than all other Studebaker products) but not enough and the line was discontinued in 1933. Named after football coach Knute Rockne.

24B: **Studebaker President Eight** seven-passenger Limousine was top-line model on 130-in. wb and powered by 5½-litre engine. Studebaker's other Eight was the Commander Series on 125-in. wb. Studebaker had started in 1852 and in 1902 had made its first (electric) car. Like most other firms it suffered badly from the Depression.

24C: **Willys-Knight Six** was Willys-Overland's last car with sleeve-valve engine. Shown is the model 66E Sedan which cost $1395. Later in the year the small and cheap Willys 77 was introduced but sales were extremely bad, mainly due to the Depression. Willys' earlier cheap car, the Whippet, had been discontinued in 1931.

24A Rockne

24B Studebaker

24C Willys

The year 1933 saw almost universal adoption of V-shaped radiator grilles, slanted windshields and other forms of streamlining. Among the technical 'novelties' were independent front suspension, valve seat inserts, reflex glass tail- and stop-lights, 'No-Draft Ventilation' with swivelling vent-windows (Fisher Bodies), use of accelerator pedal for starting and power-assisted brakes. Reo was the first with an automatic transmission. It was not a sophisticated affair, featuring only two forward ratios (Low and Direct) without the possibility of detent down shift ('kick down') but, with its big engine producing 'bags of torque' it provided effortless and sensational driving. Statistically, too, things looked a bit brighter. Car production was up by 438,021 to 1,573,512, trucks and buses by 111,358 to 346,545. The wholesale value of these 1,920,057 vehicles was $949 million, but another 4105 motor dealers had gone out of business and total car registrations were also down. Truck and bus registrations, however, were slightly up. It was about this time that White introduced its 'pancake' truck engine with twelve horizontally opposed cylinders. Ralph de Palma celebrated his 25th anniversary as a racer and Louis Meyer, driving a Miller, won the Indianapolis Sweepstakes at an average speed of 104·162 mph.

25A: **Buick Eight** with German Convertible coachwork built by Alexis Kellner of Heilbronn a/Neckar.
25B: **Buick Eight Series CA** with right-hand drive, built by General Motors of Canada Ltd as McLaughlin-Buick, for British market.
25C: **Cadillac Series 452C** touring car with 165-bhp V16 engine and 149-in. wb. Only 6654 cars were produced this year, including Series 345C and 355C V8 and 370C V12 models.
25D: **Chevrolet Master Series CA** Coupé. Standard CC had louvres in hood (instead of vent doors) and shorter wb (107 vs 110 in.). Master CA was first known as Eagle.

25A Buick

25B Buick

25C Cadillac

25D Chevrolet

26A: **Chrysler CL Custom Imperial Eight** with typical double-cowl Phaeton bodywork. Power output was 135 bhp with 5·8:1 or 125 bhp with 5·2:1 compression ratio, both at 3200 rpm. Bore and stroke were no less than $3\frac{1}{2} \times 5$ in. giving 384·8-cu in. piston displacement.

26B: **Chrysler CT Royal Eight** Sedan (top) and **Chrysler CO Six** Brougham sold at $995 and $795 respectively. There were four other body styles in the Eight series, five others in the Six.

26C: **DeSoto SD Special Six** Brougham had split windshield and forward-opening doors. The engine was the familiar L-head and in this application had $3\frac{1}{4} \times 4\frac{3}{8}$ in. bore and stroke resulting in a cubic capacity of 217·7 cu in. Wheelbase was 114 in.

26D: **Dodge DP Six** Sedan was not unlike the DeSoto but had $3\frac{1}{8}$ in. bore engine (201·3 cu in.). It was also available with eight-cylinder engine, as Model DO, with 282·1-cu in. capacity and maximum output of 100 bhp. Wheelbase 115 and 122 in.

26B Chrysler

26C DeSoto

26D Dodge

26A Chrysler

27A Essex

27B Ford

27C Ford

27A: **Essex** became **Terraplane** in 1933 (1934 in Britain). In Britain the name **Essex Terraplane** was used in 1933. Shown is **Terraplane Eight** Convertible Coupé.

27B: **Ford Model 40 V8** with Swiss Convertible bodywork. The Model 40 was also available with the old four-cylinder engine. Wheelbase was 112 in.

27C: **Ford Model 40 V8** Tudor Sedan (Body Type 700) was one of many body styles offered by the factory. The four-cylinder was similar except for V8 ornaments.

27D: **Hudson L Major Eight Brougham** was the luxurious model. Hudson's bread-and-butter lines were the popular Super Six and Essex Terraplanes (Six and Eight).

27D Hudson

1933

28A: **Hupmobile 322F Eight** Convertible Coupé had eight-in-line engine and 122-in. wb chassis. It was produced by the Hupp Motor Car Corp. which existed from 1908 until 1941.

28B: **LaSalle Series 345C V8** Sedan had the same 353-cu in. engine as Cadillac Series 355C. Like most American 1933 models it had 'skirted' front fenders (wings). Wheelbase was 136 in.

28C: **Lincoln KB V12** with Convertible bodywork. Two chassis lengths were available: 136 in. (KA, 2nd Series) and 145 in. (KB). The latter chassis was frequently used by custom body builders.

28D: **Nash Big Six 1127** Town Sedan was one of six body styles available. Engine was L-head with $3\frac{1}{4} \times 4\frac{3}{8}$ in. bore and stroke. Wheelbase 116 in. Also with 8-cyl. engine.

28C Lincoln

28A Hupmobile

28B LaSalle

28D Nash

29A: Oldsmobile F33 Six Sedan shared Fisher body styling with other General Motors products. The L33 Eight had similar bodywork with the exception of the radiator grille which had slanted bars and a different ornament on top. The cubic capacity of the two engines was 221·4 and 240·3 cu in. respectively.

29B: Packard Eight, Tenth Series, Model 1002 Sedan. This series (Jan. to Aug. 1933) also comprised Super Eight Models 1003 and 1004 and Twelve Models 1005 and 1006. The Eight had two wb sizes—$127\frac{1}{2}$ in. (1001) and 136 in. (1002, shown). Altogether Packard listed 55 body styles for the Tenth Series.

29C: Pierce-Arrow 'Silver Arrow' V12 Sedan, one of five made by hand and offered at $10,000 at Chicago World's Fair and New York Auto Show. Engine developed 175 bhp and spare wheels were in lockers behind front wheels. Note advanced styling and absence of running boards.

29B Packard

29A Oldsmobile

29C Pierce-Arrow

30A: **Plymouth PD Six** was claimed to be the 'largest six in the low-price field'. Chrysler's Plymouth concept had been well received by the public and sales were phenomenal.

30B: **Plymouth** alias **Fargo.** Chrysler's fleet and government sales being handled by the Fargo Division, Plymouth cars for the US Army and Civilian Conservation Corps were officially known as Fargos.

30C: **Pontiac 601 Eight.** In 1933 Pontiac offered only eight-cylinder models. The engine was an in-line L-head with $3\frac{3}{16} \times 3\frac{1}{2}$ in. bore and stroke, giving 223·4 cu in. piston displacement.

30D: **Pontiac 601 Eight** two-door Sedan or Coach. Other body styles included Standard, Sport and Convertible Coupés, Roadster, Four-door and Touring Sedan. Wheelbase for all models was 115 in.

30A Plymouth

30B Plymouth

30C Pontiac

30D Pontiac

31A: **Rockne Six 65** was low-price 110-in. wb car offered by Studebaker. It was sold both at home and in various export markets, in Coupé, Phaeton and Sedan (shown) form. Over 30,000 were made, selling at prices from $585 to $675.

31B: **Studebaker President Eight** Sedan used as a baker's van in the Netherlands in about 1943. Like so many cars in war-torn Europe it was converted to run on producer gas and this particular installation was rather cumbersome.

31C: **Willys Four 77** Coupé was light, cheap and not exactly elegant but sold well enough to save Willys-Overland from bankruptcy. Engine was 134-cu in. 45-bhp. A Six Model 99 was also available (213·3 cu in. 80 bhp) but not for long.

31B Studebaker

31A Rockne

31C Willys

1934 saw more streamlining and increased use of independent front suspensions. Chevrolet produced its 10 millionth car to celebrate its 23rd anniversary and nation-wide automotive production was definitely on the upswing with 2,177,919 cars and 575,192 trucks and buses. Wholesale value of replacement parts and accessories produced during this year amounted to $299,879,633—a 28% increase over 1933. The millionth Plymouth and Nash were produced (since 1928 and 1917 respectively) and world-wide Ford production during the year reached 859,526. Chrysler and DeSoto introduced the revolutionary but ill-fated 'Airflow' design with 'interlocked' body and frame and automatic Overdrive, and Graham offered a supercharged engine. Cadillac pioneered and first used a generator with controlled current to keep the battery fully charged at all times for extra loads (radio, heater). Hudson was first to introduce pinned piston rings in American cars and offered luggage compartment with concealed tyre at rear. Studebaker was the first manufacturer to use lead bronze con rod bearings and was the last to produce a Six with firing order 1–4–2–6–3–5; thereafter 1–5–3–6–2–4 became universal. Nash introduced the lower-price LaFayette car, and 'Wild Bill' Cummings averaged 104·865 mph to win Indianapolis Sweepstakes.

32A Buick

32B Buick

32A: **Buick Eight Series 90** Club Sedan with built-in trunk, Model 91, had 136-in. wb, weighed 4980 pounds and cost $1965. It was one of an entirely new range of Buicks, featuring 'knee action' front suspension.

32B: **Buick Eight Series 60** Sedan, Model 67, had 128-in. wb and sold at $1425. Other Series were 40 (117-in. wb) and 50 (119-in. wb). Lowest-priced Buick was model 46 Coupé at $795.

32C: **Cadillac Series 20 V8** Seven-passenger Sedan and Imperial Sedan had 136-in. wb and shared same Fisher bodywork. Spare wheel was concealed within the body. Other models included V12 and V16.

32C Cadillac

33A Buick

33B Chevrolet

33C Chevrolet

33D Chrysler

33A: **Buick,** built in Canada. (McLaughlin, Series NA), was quite popular in Britain where several specimens still exist. Available were Series 50 (models 50, 56, 57, 58), Series 60 (models 61, 67) and Series 90 (models 90, 91), priced upwards from £505. They remained virtually unchanged for 1935.

33B: **Chevrolet Master Series DA** Sedan. Period advertisement of Canadian-built model for the British market. First Chevrolet with Dubonnet type independent front suspension. The Standard Series DC looked rather similar but was less luxurious and had a rigid front axle; mechanically it resembled the 1933 Standard.

33C: **Chevrolet Master Series DA** Town Sedan cost $635 and featured built-in trunk (boot) and wb 2 in. longer than 1933 model. 'Blue Flame' combustion chamber design raised power output to 80 bhp at 3300 rpm. Glove compartment could now be locked with a key. Weight 3130 lb.

33D: **Chrysler CA Six** Convertible Coupé with 3·95-litre engine. This particular car was originally supplied by the Chrysler dealer in Koblenz, Germany, and came to Britain in 1946. It was completely restored in 1965—66 and is shown here at the Pre-1950 American Auto Club's 1967 rally.

34A Chrysler

34B DeSoto

34C DeSoto

34D Dodge

34A: **Chrysler Airflow CV Imperial** Sedan proved a costly 'white elephant' since it was way ahead of its time. There were also Eight (CU) and Custom Imperial (CX, CW) models.

34B: **DeSoto Airflow SE** Sedan. Other body style options: Coupé, two-door Brougham and Town Sedan. All models were powered by a 100-bhp six-cylinder L-head engine.

34C: **DeSoto Airflow SE** Town Sedan, with the famous Fokker F18 'Pelikaan' which flew from Amsterdam to Batavia (Dutch East Indies) delivering Christmas mail in 1933 in a record of four days 4½ hours.

34D: **Dodge DeLuxe DR Six** Sedan had new grille, front and rear vent windows and 117-in. wb. Engine output was 82 bhp. Also available 121-in. wb 87-bhp Six Special.

35A Ford

35C Ford

35D Ford

35B Ford

Ford Model 40 of 1934 resembled the 1933 model, except for the V8 badge on the radiator grille which was now a triangular shape (rather than 'cut-out'), the wheel hub covers and two hood handles at each side instead of one. It was also available with the four-cylinder engine. In Britain the 14·9 HP (Model 18) was continued alongside the Model 40.

35A: **Model 40 (Four)** with German bodywork by Papler. Four-cylinder models had oval Ford emblem on hub caps.

35B: **Model 40 (V8)** Sedan with sliding roof and large trunk was Dutch modification. Basically body style 730.

35C: **Model 40 (V8)** Convertible by Alexis Kellner, marketed on the Continent of Europe.

35D: **Model 40 (V8)** Roadster (710). Other Ford body styles included Coupés, Sedans (Tudor and Fordor), Victoria, Phaeton, Cabriolet.

36A

36B

36A, B, C: This 'one-off' **Ford Model 40 V8** Roadster was produced by the coach building firm of Schutter & van Bakel in Amsterdam to the design of its owner, the Dutch automotive engineer A. F. Loyens. The chassis was supplied by Ford's Amsterdam assembly plant. Mr Loyens used the car in various European countries and for a tour across the United States. Eventually he mounted the bodywork on a Hispano-Suiza chassis. Pictures show the car in France, USA (Rocky Mountains) and Switzerland. World-wide dealer network made the Ford an attractive car for such international use.

36C

36D Graham-Paige

36D: Graham-Paige 'Blue Streak' Six and Eight were in production from 1932—34, and pioneered the 'skirted fenders'. Many were exported.
36E: Hudson Eight DeLuxe Sedan had 108-bhp engine, 116-in. wb, and four forward-opening doors. Weight was 3020 lb, price $895.

36E Hudson

37A: LaSalle Series 350D Eight now had an in-line ('straight') engine and was also known as Series 50. It was produced by Cadillac on a 119-in. wb chassis with 'knee action' ifs.

37B: Lincoln KB V12 Limousine shown in typical period advertisement. Two basic models were available, the 136-in. wb KA and the 145-in. wb KB, each with a variety of standard and custom-built bodies.

37C: Nash Ambassador Eight 1290 Sedan with Charles W. Nash (left) and E. H. McCarty, president of Nash Motors. Cheapest model was LaFayette.

37D: Oldsmobile L34 Eight Sedan had Fisher bodywork with re-styled front end. The 'All Feature Six' Model F34 was almost identical in appearance. The 'Knee Action' ifs is just visible.

37A LaSalle

THE WILLOUGHBY LIMOUSINE

The LINCOLN

THE LINCOLN, a versatile car, continually astonishes loyal owners who put it to supreme tests of one kind, and then, on another occasion, find that it can meet wholly new and different tests. Thus, a rancher in Wyoming, accustomed to mountain and desert driving, learns from his wife of the car's agility in city traffic. A business man, to whom the Lincoln is a triumph of engineering, suddenly realizes, as he emerges from the opera, how beautiful a car he drives. The Lincoln is all things to all people. . . . This is a luxurious car, a safe car, with a V-12 cylinder, 150-horsepower engine powerful enough to take steep hills in high and at an almost incredible pace. Lincoln engineers affirm it the finest they have yet designed, and experience on the road confirms that judgment. And it is a car which imparts to the owner, no less than to the maker, pride in its beauty and pleasure in its high achievements. Available in twenty-three standard and custom-built body types,

37B Lincoln

37C Nash

37D Oldsmobile

38A Packard

38A: **Packard Twelve, Eleventh Series** Touring Sedan by Schutter
& van Bakel of Amsterdam, Netherlands. Note twin sliding-roof
panels and built-in trunk. The V12 engine had a bore and stroke of
$3\frac{7}{16} \times 4$ in. and developed 160 bhp at 3200 rpm. 11th Series
production span: Aug. 1933–Aug. 1934.
38B: **Packard Eight, Eleventh Series** Sedan. There were several
models, namely the 1100 (129-in. wb) Sedan, the 1101 (136-in. wb)
with eleven body styles, the 1102 (141-in. wb) with two body styles,
and the following Super Eight models: 1103 (135-in. wb) Sedan, 1104
(142-in. wb) with eleven body styles, 1105 Standard, Dietrich and
LeBaron (all 147-in. wb) with ten body styles.

38B Packard

39A Plymouth

39B Studebaker

39C Studebaker

39D Terraplane

39A: Plymouth PE DeLuxe had 113½-in. wb and independent front suspension. Models PF and PG had 107¾-in. wb. All had 201-cu in. L-head Six engine. In August the one millionth Plymouth was made.

39B: Studebaker Commander Regal Eight Convertible with bodywork by Alexis Kellner exhibited in Dutch dealer's showroom. Body is strikingly similar to that of Pennock and other firms, including some in Great Britain.

39C: Studebaker Commander Regal Eight 119-in. wb chassis with Dutch Convertible bodywork by Pennock of The Hague. This type of body was built on various American chassis by several European firms.

39D: Terraplane Six Convertible Coupé was entirely new and in styling looked much like its parent Hudson. Characteristic for 1934 model year was upright louvres in hood (bonnet) sides.

Combined motor vehicle production during 1935 was not far below the four million mark. Total car, truck and bus registrations were the highest since 1930, at 26,227,000. Some three million autos now had radios and an AMA report disclosed that motorists now paid one of every eight tax dollars. 172,572 cars and chassis were exported. Technically there were few innovations but there was a trend toward two- and four-door Sedans and lower-priced less luxurious models with less powerful engines. Cadillac's medium-priced LaSalle, like most other GM products, now featured Fisher Bodies' 'Turret Top', which was an all-steel roof. Chrysler Corporation, smallest of the 'Big Three', exceeded its 1929 sales record for the third year in succession, although their total unit sales (Chrysler, DeSoto, Dodge and Plymouth) was well below that of Chevrolet and Ford. General Motors during 1935 recorded a total sales to dealers of 1,715,688 units, ranging from the cheapest Chevvy at $495 to the top-line Cadillac at $7750. Of this total, just over one million were Chevrolets. It was the Chevrolet Division's first million-plus year since 1929. Packard announced its low-price One Twenty car and saw annual production increase from 5,818 in 1934 to 52,256. Pontiac delivered its one millionth car (since 1926). The Ford Motor Company introduced its Lincoln Zephyr and participated in the 1935 National Automobile Show after having ignored national shows since early in the century. Nash offered a new type of 'seal-in' engine which meant that the conventional manifolding was cast inside the cylinder block.

40A Auburn

40B Auburn

40C Buick

40D Buick

40A: Auburn 851 Supercharged Speedster was impressive 100-mph machine with a straight-eight 150-bhp Lycoming engine. Fitted with supercharger and two-speed rear axle it was also available with other body styles.

40B: Auburn supplied six- and eight-cylinder models and they were also available in Britain as this period advertisement shows. Illustrated is the model 653 Sedan which cost £399. Wheelbase was 120 in.

40C: Buick Eight NA Series Convertible Coupé with rumble seat, model 56C, built in Canada for British market where it sold at £500. Price in the USA was $1230.

40D: Buick Eight NA Series Sedan. 1935 models were substantially the same as 1934. Most Buicks sold in Britain (with rhd) were produced in Canada and technically were McLaughlin-Buicks.

41A Chevrolet

41A: **Chevrolet Master Series EA** Coach with Dubonnet 'Knee Action' ifs and Fisher 'turret top' body. Master ED had rigid front axle.

41B: **Chevrolet Standard Series EC** resembled 1934 Standard DC and was continued as an economy model. Period advertisement lists Canadian products.

41C: **Chrysler Airstream** range was much more salable than contemporary Airflow models. In Britain they were known as 'Airglide Kingston'

41D: British **Chrysler Airflow** of 1935 was in fact 1934 DeSoto Airflow with 1935 model SG grille and 1934 Chrysler Airflow bumpers. They were assembled by Chrysler Motors Ltd in Kew, Surrey. The car shown is a rare survivor of this equally rare model.

41C Chrysler

41B Chevrolet

41D Chrysler

42A Chrysler

42A: British **Chrysler Airflow** shown in this advertisement, which appeared at Motor Show time in October 1934, in fact shows what a 1934 DeSoto Airflow Coupé is. Components for British-assembled Chrysler products came from Canada but the end products differed from the American models in many details.

42B: **Chrysler Heston Airflow Eight** was the British designation for this 1934 Chrysler Airflow Eight. The advert appeared on the occasion of the Scottish Motor Show in November 1934. American Chrysler Airflow 1935 was face-lifted 1934 with Airstream-type grille.

42C: **DeSoto SF Airstream Six** had basically the same bodywork as the Chrysler Airstream. Body styles included Sedan (shown), Roadster and Coupé.

42D: **DeSoto SG Airflow Six** came in three models: Coupé, four-door Sedan (shown) and Town Sedan. Wheelbase was $115\frac{1}{2}$ in., piston displacement 241·5 cu in. ($B \times S$ $3\frac{3}{8} \times 4\frac{1}{2}$ in.) and power output 100 bhp at 3400 rpm. Front axle was rigid with leaf springs.

42B Chrysler

42C DeSoto

42D DeSoto

43A Dodge

43B Dodge

43C Ford

43D Ford

43A: **Dodge DU Six** was only 1935 Dodge model, with choice of various body styles. Engine was 3569-cc L-head (export option: DV 2794-cc).

43B: British **Dodge 'Jubilee Six'** series comprised 25.3 HP Senior Six (3569-cc) and 19.8 HP Victory Six (small-bore 2794-cc).

43C: **Ford Model 48** (V8, 3.6-litre, 30HP) and British **Model 60** (V8, 2.2-litre, 22HP) looked identical. Wheelbase was 112 in.

43D: **Ford V8** Special coachbuilt seven-seater limousine was offered 'finished to your choice' by W. Harold Perry Ltd of London N. 12.

43E: **Graham** offered various six- and eight-cylinder models but during 1935 the Eight was replaced by a supercharged Six.

43E Graham

AN EXCEPTIONALLY WIDE RANGE OF MODELS

Hudson built cars have attracted world wide admiration for their uncanny silence and brilliant performance. Further distinctiveness is given to Terraplane and Hudson cars by the wide range of models and coachwork that is available, enabling the buyer to choose the model that exactly meets his requirements. A few popular designs are here illustrated.

FOUR DOOR SALOON

Terraplanes from £299
Hudsons   „   £360

FIXED HEAD COUPE
(with dickey)

Hudson 8 £395

CONVERTIBLE COUPE
(with dickey)

Terraplane £345
Hudson 8 £410

SPECIAL OPEN SPORTS

Terraplane £375

DROP-HEAD FOURSOME

Terraplane £425
Hudson 8 £495

For particulars of other styles write to :—

HUDSON MOTORS LIMITED
Great West Road, London, W.4 (Chiswick 4777)
West End Showrooms: Shaw & Kilburn Ltd.
117 Great Portland Street, W.1

TERRAPLANE & HUDSON

44A Hudson

44A: **Hudson** and **Terraplane** came in a wide variety of models including a Panel Delivery Van. Period advertisement shows some of the models offered on the British market including British special open sports and drophead bodywork on certain chassis (see also page 47).

44B: **Hudson Six** Sedan. In 1935 Hudson introduced the 'Electric Hand' finger-tip control for gear shifting. Year's sales included 101,080 cars and 1281 commercial vehicles. The company reported that it now had 3225 Hudson-Terraplane dealers in the United States.

44C: **Hudson Eight DeLuxe Brougham** was top-line model which in Britain was offered at £499, including radio, in December 1934. 'Glide uphill at eighty miles an hour or more without a trace of mechanical noise to mar your enjoyment'.

44B Hudson

44C Hudson

45A: **Hupmobile** offered six- and eight-cylinder models, all featuring new 'Aerodynamic' streamline styling. The hood and headlamp styling were soon to be copied in Europe by Opel and Renault.

45B: **Hupmobile** six-cylinder Sedan, surviving in Holland. Larger Sixes and Eights had a three-piece windshield; all had a two-piece rear window.

45C: **LaFayette Six** was low-price line of Nash, 1934–39. In 1935 there were eight body styles, all on 113-in. wb chassis.

45D: **LaSalle Series 50 Eight** Convertible did not differ much from 1934 model year, the main exterior difference being styling of bumpers.

45E: **Lincoln KB V12 Touring** was seven-passenger 'Royalty Special' on 145-wb chassis. Peculiar side windows retracted in the doors.

45F: **Nash** in 1935 had 'Aeroform' styling and offered only two- and four-door Sedans (Advanced Six and Eight and Ambassador Eight). 1936 models were substantially similar. Illustrated is a Model 3640 Sedan, which was available with or without trunk (built-out-boot). In 1935 Nash Motors produced a total of 44,637 Nashes and LaFayettes. In 1936 the Figure was 53,038.

45A Hupmobile

45B Hupmobile

45D LaSalle

45E Lincoln

45C LaFayette

45F Nash

46A: Oldsmobile F35 Six and L35 Eight featured Fisher 'Turret Top' all-steel roof, in common with most other GM cars from the 1935 model year.

46B: Packard One Twenty (120A), Twelfth Series Touring Sedan, body style 892. Six alternative body types. 8-in-line engine, developing 110 bhp. Wheelbase 120 in.

46C: Packard Eight 1201, Twelfth Series Convertible Victoria, body style 807. Wheelbase 134 in. (Model 1200: 127 in., Model 1202: 139 in.). Also Super Eight and Twelve ranges of models.

46D: Packard One Twenty was Packard's entry into the low-price field. Prices started at $980 (Business Coupé). Just under 25,000 produced, many for export.

46C Packard

46A Oldsmobile

46B Packard

46D Packard

47A Plymouth

47A: **Plymouth PJ Six DeLuxe** Sedan was one of Chrysler's best selling models. Marketed in Britain as Chrysler Kew Six (2794 cc, 19·8 HP) and Wimbledon Six (3298 cc, 23·4 HP).
47B: **Pontiac 701 Six** Sedan was one of seven body styles available in 1935. Eight-cylinder versions (Series 605) were also available. Bodies by Fisher, Dubonnet-type ifs.
47C: **Studebaker Commander Eight** Sedan. Car shown has non-original headlamps. Other 1935 'Studes' included Dictator and President with various body styles topped by Land Cruiser Sedans.
47D: **Terraplane Six** was popular in Hudson's home and export markets, including Britain where this Sedan sold at around £300. Engine was 2597-cc 16·9 HP or 3455-cc 21·6 HP (Big Six).
47E: **Terraplane Six** Panel Delivery was basically passenger car with modified rear body. Hudson Motor Co. produced light commercial vehicles from 1929 (Dover) until 1947.

47B Pontiac

47C Studebaker

47D Terraplane

47E Terraplane

Sales this year increased again, final production figures showing 3,669,528 cars (about 95% of which were priced below $750 wholesale) and 784,587 trucks and buses. Wholesale value of replacement parts and accessories also rose again, by 21·5%. Exports of cars and chassis totalled 179,957 units. Buick produced its three millionth car and offered flashing direction indicators (turn signals) incorporated in the transparent red plastic 'wings' of the Buick emblem on the trunk (boot) lid. Chevrolet produced over 1¼ million cars and trucks, including the firm's 12 millionth vehicle. This GM division led the industry in sales for the eighth time in 10 years and their dealer profits reached a new all-time high. The Chrysler Corporation sold more than one million vehicles for the first time in its history. Hudson patented its 'Triple-Safe' brake system and produced 123,266 cars. Most of these were Terraplanes (93,309) which came in 27 models starting with a Business Coupé at $695. It was Hudson's peak year of the decade. Nash, of Kenosha, merged with the Kelvinator Corp. of Detroit and became the Nash-Kelvinator Corp. Packard introduced its Six '110', the lowest priced Packard ever offered, and saw sales jump to over 80,000 units. For Studebaker 1936 marked the sharpest increase in business in the firm's history: car sales went up by 71·5%, trucks by 26·5%. Willys-Overland was re-organised and as Willys-Overland Motors Inc. introduced its new little 'Surprise Car of the Year', at the New York Auto Show in November (*see* 1937).

48A: **Auburn** Phaeton as produced during 1935 and 1936. Car shown was experimentally fitted with a diesel engine by the Cummins Engine Company in 1935, replacing the original 'Straight 8'.

48B: **Buick Eight** with custom-built Convertible bodywork by Schutter & van Bakel of Amsterdam. American GM cars for the Benelux countries were (and are) mostly assembled by General Motors Continental S.A. in Antwerp.

48C: **Buick Eight Series 90 Limited** Eight-passenger Sedan with built-in trunk (Model 90) was one of Buick's top-line models. A six-seater (91) and a Limousine (90L) were also available.

48B Buick

48A Auburn

48C Buick

49A: **Buick Eight Series 90** Limousine as used by the Duke of Windsor (then King Edward VIII). Like the Series 60 Century and 80 Roadmaster it had an in-line ohv engine rated at 37·8 HP.

49B: Interior of the **Buick 90** Limousine provided a high degree of privacy. Once the Duke of Windsor's private car, it was auctioned in 1969 and commanded a price of £2,300.

49C: **Cadillac V8** came in three Series: 60 (shown), 70 and 75 with wb lengths of 121, 131 and 138 in. respectively. Series 80 and 85 were V12, Series 90 was V16.

49D: **Cadillac** Limousine used by the late Princess (then Queen) Wilhelmina of the Netherlands had various modifications. In the USA this year 48·1% of all cars sold above $1500 were Cadillacs.

49C Cadillac

49A Buick

49B Buick

49D Cadillac

50A: **Chevrolet Master** had Dubonnet ifs (Series FA) or rigid front axle (FD). Cheaper FC Standard Series had similar bodywork but 109— (vs 113—) in. wb and 5·25 (vs 5·50)×17 tyres.

50B: **Chevrolet Master Imperial** was GM Continental's lwb (124 in.) model, shod with 6·00×17 tyres. Shown is the Cabriolet.

50C: **Chevrolet Standard FC** Cabriolet (one of seven FC body options) shared 206-cu in. 'Stove Bolt Six' with FA and FD Series.

50D: British **Chrysler Wimbledon Six Airglide** was basically a Plymouth. Other 1935 British Chryslers: Kew, Richmond and Croydon (all Sixes), Heston Airflow 8 and Royal Airflow. Prices £289—£725.

1936 BRINGS YOU ALL THE GOOD THINGS OF MOTORING

MADE IN CANADA

AT A PRICE YOU CAN AFFORD MODELS FROM **£268**

50A Chevrolet

50B Chevrolet

50C Chevrolet

50D Chrysler

51A: Chrysler C8 DeLuxe Eight Town Sedan by LeBaron, preserved in the National Automobile Museum at Leidschendam, Holland (photo: Lex W. Klimbie). C7 Series had similar front end but six-cylinder engine and different louvres in hood.

51B: Chrysler C9 Airflow Eight Sedan. Other 1936 Chrysler Airflows were the C10 Imperial and C11 Custom Imperial. Model shown had $122\frac{13}{16}$-in. wb and 323·5-cu in. 115-bhp in-line engine.

51C: DeSoto S1 Custom Airstream Six Sedan. Also available was a DeLuxe Airstream which had single-piece windshield. Technically the DeSoto, Dodge and Plymouth (all Chrysler products) had much in common.

51D: DeSoto S2 Airflow Sedan was also available in two-door form, termed Coupé. 5000 S2 cars were built in this, the last year of the DeSoto Airflows.

51A Chrysler

51B Chrysler

51C DeSoto

51D DeSoto

52A: **Dodge D2 Six** Sedan was marketed in Great Britain as Senior Six Saloon or Limousine. Coupés were also offered.

52B: **Dodge D2 Six** had 87-bhp 3·57-litre L-head engine (25·3 HP) but for export a smaller-bore edition (23·4 HP) was available, designated D3. Note sidemounts on this surviving Sedan.

52C: **Fargo FD1-16** was attractive looking Parcel Van based on Chrysler Plymouth car chassis. Chrysler used Fargo name for certain commercial, export and military vehicles.

52D: **Ford Model 68 V8** had 112-in. wb and the catalogue listed 16 body styles including this Type 760 Cabriolet. They all had the 3·6-litre (30HP) engine.

52E: **Ford Model 68 V8** Station Wagon, Type 790, shared its sheet metal with the passenger cars but was catalogued in Ford's Commercial and Truck range.

53A: **Graham Series 110 Supercharger Six** models were introduced in 1935, replacing the former Eight models. Eight, however, was still available in Britain by mid-1936.

53B: **International C-1** with taxicab bodywork for use in Norway. 'Airwheels' had 7·00 × 15 tyres. Basically this was a 125-in. wb light truck chassis.

53C: **LaFayette Six 3618** was four-door Sedan made by Nash on 113-in. wb and billed as 'the big car in the low price field'.

52A Dodge

52B Dodge

52C Fargo

52D Ford

52E Ford

53D: **LaSalle Series 50 Eight** Coupé with 120-in. wb. This was the last year in which Cadillac produced an in-line Eight. Typical list price $1225.

53E: **Lincoln Zephyr Model H V12** was first introduced by the Ford Motor Co. for the 1936 model year. This ultra-streamlined 122-in. wb Sedan was 202½ in. long.

53F: **Lincoln KA** Phaeton featured 67° V12 engine with $3\frac{1}{8} \times 4\frac{1}{2}$ in. bore and stroke giving a piston displacement of 414 cu in. Compression ratio was 5·25:1, output 150 bhp at 3400 rpm.

53G: **Nash DeLuxe 400 Six** two-door Sedan model 3645A had 117-in. wb. Ambassador Six and Super Eight had 125-in. wb. Total Nash sales: 53,038.

53A Graham

53C LaFayette

53B International

53F Lincoln

53D LaSalle

53E Lincoln

53G Nash

54A: **Oldsmobile F36 Six and L36 Eight** had open coil spring ifs and wb sizes of 115 and 121 in. respectively. A wide range of all-steel Fisher bodies was available.

54B: **Packard Super Eight, Fourteenth Series** was in production from August 1935 until September 1936. There were three models, 1403 (132-in. wb), 1404 (139-in. wb) and 1405 (144-in. wb) with 17 body styles.

54C: **Pierce-Arrow 1601 Eight** Club Sedan with 144-in. wb chassis had 150-bhp engine plus power brakes with vacuum booster and a host of other safety features and luxury fittings. 1602 and 1603 were V12s.

54D: **Plymouth P1 Six** Station Wagon could carry seven to eight passengers. Also available on the same 113-in. wb chassis was a steel-panelled Commercial Sedan (also known as Sedan Delivery).

54A Oldsmobile

54B Packard

54C Pierce-Arrow

54D Plymouth

55A: **Pontiac Master and DeLuxe Six and Eight** had Dubonnet type ifs, L-head (side-valve) engines of 27·4 and 33·8 HP rating and 'Silver Streak' bodywork by Fisher.

55B: **Pontiac Eight Silver Streak** two-door Sedan, was one of seven body styles available on the Eight with 116⅝-in. wb and also on the Six (Master and DeLuxe) with 112-in. wb.

55C: **Terraplane Six** was shaped like the contemporary Hudson but lower in price. Wheelbase was 115 in. and engine output 88 bhp with an optional 100. Two-door Sedan version was termed Brougham.

55D: **Terraplane Six** Station Wagon helped Hudson Motor Co. to increase sales to almost 25% above the previous year. All doors were forward-opening. Wheels were 'easy-clean' type.

55A Pontiac

55B Pontiac

55C Terraplane

55D Terraplane

1937

1937 saw another increase in US motor vehicle sales: 3,915,889 cars, and 893,085 trucks and buses. Ford could claim highest total sales (although Chevrolet sold more cars, Ford sold more trucks, just enough to beat Chevrolet's overall figure). The battle for leadership between Ford and Chevrolet was always fierce. It is interesting to compare these two cars, technically. In 1937 their share of overall US car sales was: Chevrolet 22·05%, Ford 21·99%. Yet, compared with the present time, these two cars were different in so many respects that millions of people had developed a kind of loyalty towards either one or the other. Ford introduced a V8 engine in 1932 whereas Chevrolet had built Sixes ever since 1929 and did not offer an optional V8 until 1955 (except for a few in 1917–19). Fords had alligator-type hoods (bonnets) and built-in headlamps from 1937, Chevrolet not until 1940–41. Fords had a manual starter from 1937, Chevrolet stuck to a pedal until 1949. Other characteristic Ford features were their split-type rear axle, side valves, round pedal pads, steering column-mounted ignition switch (1932–48) and transversal road springs with 'live' front axle (1906–48). Chevrolets had longitudinal leaf springs with ifs on top-line models from 1934 (all from 1941), banjo-type rear axles, overhead valves and oblong pedal pads. Number three US car, Chrysler's Plymouth (13·27% of 1937 total sales) was different again and some of its distinguishing features were a side-valve Six engine with high-up starter pedal, parking brake behind the gearbox, open prop shaft and semi-elliptics all round (until 1939). Each of these three marques had its own individual 'personality' with distinguishing engine sound, handling and 'feel'.

56A Buick

56A: Buick Eight Series 60 Century Touring Sedan model 61 with trunk and fender well. In the USA this 3975-lb car cost $1105 Six other body styles, including Convertible Phaeton.
56B: Canadian **Buick (McLaughlin) Series CO** with British Albemarle Drop Head Coupé bodywork. 1937 Buick series and wb lengths: 40 Special (122 in.), 60 Century (126 in.), 80 Roadmaster (131 in.), 90 Limited (138 in.).
56C: **Cadillac V8** came in four series and wb lengths, namely 60 (124 in.), 65 (131 in.), 70 (131 in.) and 75 (138 in.). In addition there were the 85 (V12, 138 in.) and 90 (V16, 154 in.), and LaSalle 50 (V8, 124 in.). Shown: Series 70.

56B Buick

56C Cadillac

57A: **Chevrolet 'Cheetah'** was Canadian export model with 81 instead of 88·9 mm cylinder bore, resulting in 24·4 instead of 29·3 HP treasury rating. It was available in the UK only during 1937 and part of 1938.

57B: **Chevrolet Master DeLuxe Series GA** with custom-built coachwork by van Rijswijk in the Netherlands. Series GA had Dubonnet ifs; Master Series GB had rigid front axle, otherwise basically similar.

57C: **Chrysler Imperial Eight** was top-line model. Car shown was seen in Spain, powered by a Barreiros diesel engine, in the 1960s.

57D: **Cord 812,** shown with some later modifications, was powered by Lycoming L-head V8 engine, driving the front wheels. Headlamps were retractable. Also available with closed bodywork. First introduced in 1935 (810). Power output (with supercharger) was 195 bhp.

57B Chevrolet

57A Chevrolet

57C Chrysler

57D Cord

58A: **Chrysler Airflow C17.** This was the last Airflow car. It had an 8-cyl. 323-cu in. engine and 128-in. wb. Total Airflow output from 1934 was 29,928 Chryslers, 25,737 DeSotos.

58B: **DeSoto S3 DeLuxe Six** had 3·74-litre 93-bhp power unit and 116-in. wb (except Seven-Place Sedan shown, which had 133-in. wb and glass partition). Other body styles included two- and four-door Sedans, Convertible Sedan and various Coupés.

58C: **DeSoto SP Six** was special export model with four body styles (Sedan, Touring Sedan, Two-door Sedan, Coupé with Dickey-Seat) and was in effect a slightly modified Plymouth. It had a 3·3-litre 78-bhp L-head engine and wb was 112 in.

58D: **Dodge D5 DeLuxe Six** had 3·6-litre engine and 116- or 133-in. wb. Available for export was a 112-in. wb model (Dodge D6 Six or Victory) which had a smaller-bore 3·3 litre engine. Like the DeSoto SP this smaller Dodge was basically a Plymouth.

58A Chrysler

58B DeSoto

58C DeSoto

58D Dodge

59A Ford

59B Ford

59C Ford

59D Hudson

59E LaFayette

59F LaSalle

59A: **Ford V8 models 74 and 78** were identical in appearance except for V8 badge on radiator grille which showed engine type fitted: 60-bhp 2·2-litre for Model 74, 85-bhp 3·6-litre for Model 78. In Britain the former was largely supplanted by the smaller Model 62 (see 75C).

59B: **Ford V8 Model 78** with van bodywork, operated by the YMCA during World War 2. It was one of numerous passenger cars which were converted in 1939/40 to serve as ambulances, tea and food vans, entertainment and library vans, etc. These vehicles were invariably crewed by women volunteers.

59C: **Ford V8 Model 78** Station Wagon as produced by Ford of Britain. Officially termed Utility, these models were popularly known as 'Woodies'. Note modified headlamps.

59D: **Hudson Eight** Convertible Brougham. Optional equipment included the 'Electric Hand' automatic gear shift. Hudson Eights were available with two wb lengths, 122 and 129 in.

59E: **LaFayette** two-door Sedan, Model 3713, was low-price offering by Nash, selling at $655 fob Kenosha, Wisc. In 1937 Nash merged with Kelvinator, forming Nash-Kelvinator Corp.

59F: **LaSalle Series 50 V8** Coupé. After three years of straight eights, the LaSalle was powered by a V8 engine again. Wheelbase was 124 in., typical list price $1260.

60A Lincoln

60B Lincoln

60A: **Lincoln Zephyr HB V12** Two-door Sedan, fitted with sunroof (Dutch modification). As can be seen, the European Ford V8 models (page 75) had several styling features in common with the Zephyr.

60B: **Lincoln Zephyr HB V12** Coupé had exceptionally long 'rear deck'. Note also the streamlined rear light units and the rear wheel cover panels which came as standard equipment. Wb was 122 in.

60C: **Nash Ambassador Eight** Sedan, Model 3788, was priced at ＄945 and is shown here with the famous baseball player Babe Ruth.

60D: **Oldsmobile F37 Six and L37 Eight** shared Fisher bodyshells with contemporary Buicks and Pontiacs. These were different from those used by Chevrolet. Olds Six and Eight wb was 117 and 124 in. respectively. Shown: L37 Eight Touring Sedan.

60C Nash

60D Oldsmobile

61A Packard

61B Packard

61C Packard

61A: Packard Eight (One Twenty), Fifteenth Series, Model 120C Convertible Coupé. Wheelbase 120 in. Nine body styles.

61B: Packard Super Eight, Fifteenth Series, Model 1501 Club Sedan. Wheelbase 134 in. Engine: 135 bhp at 3200 rpm.

61C: Packard Super Eight, Fifteenth Series, Model 1500 Touring Sedan. Wheelbase 127 in. Model 1502 had 139-in. wb.

61D: Packard Six (One Ten), Fifteenth Series, Model 115C (110) Four-door Sedan was one of eight body styles available on this 115-in. wb chassis. L-head engine developed 100 bhp.

61E: Plymouth Six Photo shows Mr Piet Olyslager as free-lance motoring journalist with DeLuxe Sedan on Mont Ventoux, France. In Britain this model was named Chrysler Kew Six.

61D Packard

61E Plymouth

62A: **Pontiac Silver Streak** was again available as either a Six (wb 117 in.) or Eight (wb 122 in.). There were eight common body styles. Station Wagon came only as Six.

62B: **Pontiac Silver Streak** was also available in Britain, with right-hand drive. Silver Streak name indicated Pontiac's characteristic band of chrome mouldings over grille and hood.

62C: **Studebaker Six and Eight** were offered in Great Britain, starting from £458. The model shown in this advertisement of July 1937 shows convertible coachwork by Salmons.

62D: **Studebaker President Eight** had 4·1-litre engine and 125- or 143-in. wb. Dictator Six models had 3·6-litre engine, 116-in. wb. Windshield washers were offered for the first time.

62A Pontiac

62C Studebaker

62B Pontiac

62D Studebaker

63A: **Terraplane Panel Delivery** was based on Hudson's Terraplane car chassis. A total of 111,342 vehicles were produced in Hudson's Detroit plants during this year. 8,058 of these were commercial vehicles. Hudson was one of the first American manufacturers to locate the battery in the engine compartment, making it more accessible.

63B: **Terraplane DeLuxe Six** Sedan Model 71 was popular in Great Britain and a survivor is shown here at a recent rally of the Pre-50 American Auto Club. In this year Hudson made the ash tray standard equipment and dropped the rumble seat option on Coupés. For 1938 Terraplane became Hudson Terraplane.

63C: **Willys-Overland Four** was completely restyled and had 100-in. wb chassis with various body options such as Sedan (shown), Coupé, Roadster and Tourer. The WW II Jeep's 'Go Devil' engine was developed from the power unit of these cars. In Australia the Willys was available with locally made Sedan body.

63B Terraplane

63A Terraplane

63C Willys

Following ever-increasing sales figures since the 1932 slump, 1938 was a shattering set-back, with production down by 40%. More than one million fewer cars found customers than in 1937 and truck and bus production was down by almost half. The number of motor dealers had been on the increase since 1932 but towards the year's end had fallen again sharply. At the end of the year, however, business picked up again. Chevrolet's sales to dealers were down from 1,189,016 to 694,039 units. Chrysler put it like this: 'Sales and earnings for the year 1938 reflected the fact that business generally suffered a precipitate decline from the preceeding three years'. The Corporation produced only 570,852 units (less than half the 1937 output) but spent $18 million on improving its facilities, including the completion of a new truck plant. Chrysler also introduced a fluid coupling which 'eliminated all metal-to-metal contact between the engine and driving wheels'. Ford spent $40 million for plant expansion and introduced the Mercury. Several car makers, including Buick, Cadillac and Pontiac introduced steering column-mounted gear shift lever (1939 models).

64B Buick

64A Buick

64C Cadillac

64A: **Buick Eight Series 60 Century** Sport Coupé, Model 66S, had 'Opera Seat' in rear of passenger compartment. 'Dynaflash' valve-in-head engine produced 141 bhp.
64B: **Buick Eight CO Series** Convertible Coupé of Canadian origin. Buick's 1938 range with four Series was much the same as 1937 but grilles had fewer bars.
64C: **Cadillac Series 65 V8** Touring Sedan. 1938 range comprised Series 60 (124-in. wb), 60S (126-in. wb), 65 (132-in. wb) and 75 (141-in. wb) as well as V16 Series 90.
64D: **Cadillac V8** with standard Coupé bodywork by Fisher. The V12 was discontinued. A total of 24,950 Cadillacs and LaSalles were sold in 1938 (46,153 in 1937).

64D Cadillac

65A: **Cadillac Series 90 V16** was the most expensive model and sold at well over $5000. Cadillac was first with 135° V-type 16-cylinder engine.

65B: **Chevrolet Master DeLuxe Series HA** Town Sedan. The Master HB was a less luxurious version with rigid front axle. Series 018 Master Taxicab was also available.

65C: **Chrysler Royal Six** Sedan with 119-in. wb. Also available as 136-in. wb Seven-Place Sedan or Limousine. Larger Chryslers were the Imperial and Custom Imperial Eights.

65D: **DeSoto Six** came in two basic variants: S5 (119- or 136-in. wb) and SP5 (export, 112-in. wb).

65E: **DeSoto S5 Custom Six** resembled Chrysler Royal and Dodge in many respects.

65C Chrysler

65A Cadillac

65D DeSoto

65B Chevrolet

65E DeSoto

66A: **Dodge D8 DeLuxe Six** Convertible Coupé was one of ten models available in this 3·5-litre range. Wheelbase 115 and 132 in.

66B: **Dodge D8 Custom Six** Sedan. A smaller model, the D9 with 112-in. wb,. was available for export. Treasury rating 25·35 and 19·8 HP respectively.

66C: **Fargo FJ1 Six** light truck chassis with 9·00 × 13 'desert tyres', one of more than 1000 delivered to Egypt. Incorporated many car components. Wheelbase 116 in.

66D: **Ford V8 Model 81A Standard 85HP** and **Model 82A 60HP** had 1937 style bodywork with revised grille. Wheelbase was 112 in. Tudor Sedan (700C) shown.

66E: **Ford V8 Model 81A DeLuxe 85 HP** with elegant Convertible bodywork made in Germany. Also available in the Netherlands. Note rear wheel shields.

66F: **Ford V8 Model 81A DeLuxe 85HP** Convertible Coupé (706A). 85 HP was also referred to as 90HP in Ford literature. In UK it was the '30HP'.

66A Dodge

66B Dodge

66C Fargo

66D Ford

66E Ford

66F Ford

67A: **Graham Super Custom 120 Six** Four-door Sedan with the front wings modified to take later type lamps. Without running boards and bumpers this car was still in use in Czechoslovakia thirty years afterwards. The unusual 'shark nose' body design was the work of Amos Northup.

67B: **Hudson Terraplane Six** Sedan with 117-in. wb and L-head (side valve) engine of 16·9 HP (2723 cc) or 21·6 HP (3475 cc) RAC rating.

67C: **Hudson Terraplane Six** DeLuxe Convertible Brougham. With a 6·25:1 compression ratio the power unit developed 101 bhp. Wheelbase 117 in.

67D: **Hudson 112 Six** was new low-priced series introduced early in 1938 and mounted on a wheelbase of 112 in.

67E: **LaSalle Series 50 V8** Covertible Coupé looked like Cadillac but had narrower radiator grille. Wheelbase measured 124 in. Bodywork by Fisher.

67A Graham

67B Hudson

67C Hudson

67D Hudson

67E LaSalle

68A: **Lincoln Zephyr 86H V12** was available in Britain with five body styles, namely Coupé Sedan, Limousine, Convertible Coupé and Convertible Sedan. Treasury HP rating was 36·3.
68B: **Lincoln Zephyr 86H V12** differed from preceding model HB mainly in that the front end was completely restyled. Wheel- and springbase were increased by 3 in.
68C: **Oldsmobile L38 Eight** Four-door Sedan had 4213-cc engine of 33·8 HP (RAC). This rhd model sold in Britain at £515 (£415 for chassis only).
68D: **Oldsmobile F38 Six** Coupé with non-standard bumpers. Exterior difference between Six and Eight was in styling of radiator grille. Engine was 3764-cc (28·3 HP RAC).

68A Lincoln

68B Lincoln

68C Oldsmobile

68D Oldsmobile

69A Packard

69A: **Packard Eight, Sixteenth Series Model 1601** Convertible Coupé on 127-in. wb chassis. Other Eight models were the 1601D and 1602 (139- and 148-in. wb). Eights were priced from $1225 up to $5100. The Six (1600) models had 122-in. wb and were priced from just below the $1000 mark.

69B: **Packard Super Eight, Sixteenth Series, Model 1603** Four-door Touring Sedan. The Super Eight was available with 127-, 134- and 139-in, wb lengths and with the exception of the 127-in. wb Sedan, body style availability was much the same as for the Twelve models. Eight and Super Eight models included custom-built bodies by Brunn and Rollson.

69C: **Packard Twelve, Sixteenth Series, Model 1608** with Dutch custom-built convertible coachwork (Schutter & van Bakel, Amsterdam). These V12 models had a 175-bhp side-valve engine with $3\frac{7}{16} \times 4\frac{1}{4}$ in. bore and stroke. Taxable horsepower was 56·7 HP (AMA). Only 566 were produced from September 1937 until September 1938 and the factory offered fourteen body styles on chassis with 134 or 139 in. wb. Prices varied from $4135 for a Model 1607 2 + 2-seater Coupé with 134-in. wb to $8510 for either a Touring or All-Weather Cabriolet, both executed by Brunn on 139-in. wb chassis.

69B Packard

69C Packard

70A: **Plymouth P6 DeLuxe Six** Sedan had 113-in. wb and was also available as Business Six, with 112-in. wb. Engines: 3·3-litre (23·4 HP) or 2·8-litre (19·8 HP; export). UK nomenclature: Chrysler Kew.

70B: **Pontiac Silver Streak Six and Eight** were very similar in appearance. This is a Six (222·7-cu in.) Four-door Sedan with 117-in. wb. Eight had 122-in. wb.

70C: **Pontiac Six** Coupé was available as Business Coupé or Sports Coupé with so-called 'Opera Seats'. Except for Six Station Wagon, all models were also available as Eights (248·9 cu in.).

70D: **Pontiac** with a difference. This auto was customised and featured modified front and rear end, lockers in front wings, full instrumentation etc. Picture taken in England, 1967.

70A Plymouth

70B Pontiac

70C Pontiac

70D Pontiac

71A: **Studebaker** period advertisement of
May 1938. Model ranges: Commander, State
Commander and State President Eight. US prices
(for Cruiser Sedans): $965, $1040 and $1205
respectively.

71B: **Studebaker State Commander Six**
featured vacuum-actuated gearshift (control on
dashboard), freewheel transmission and automatic hillholder as standard equipment.
Commander models had conventional (round)
headlamps.

71C: **Willys-Overland** was one of the smallest
US cars and many of the year's production
total of 26,673 were exported. Engine was
economical 2·2-litre L-head.

71B Studebaker

CHOOSE YOUR CAR AS CAREFULLY AS YOU CHOOSE YOUR HOME

71A Studebaker

71C Willys

This year saw several US automotive milestones. Ford produced its 27 millionth vehicle, Chevrolet its 15 millionth and the nation its 75 millionth. Car and truck/bus production rose to 2,866,796 and 710,496 respectively. Buick now offered 30 models from $894 to $2453 and introduced a sunshine roof. Chrysler was closed down for 54 days by a strike but nevertheless had the fourth best year in its history thus far. Hudson introduced 'Airfoam' seat cushions, 'Autopoise' control, helping to keep the front wheels automatically on true course, and front-hinged hood with lock release under the dashboard. Nash built its 100,000th car with 'Conditioned Air Unit'. Oldsmobile increased sales volume by more than 37% and later in the year announced the first 'Hydra-Matic' fully-automatic transmission (in 1937 Buick and Olds had introduced an automatic gear changer called 'Automatic Safety Transmission'; this system used brake bands and plate clutches but had no fluid coupling and was not available for export). Packard, in addition to turning out 76,366 cars, designed, developed and produced a high-speed marine engine for the US Navy. Studebaker introduced its new low-price Champion which was an important factor in their 117% increase in the year's unit sales. Practically all US cars now had the gear shift lever on the steering column, either as standard or as optional equipment. The electrically actuated Borg-Warner Overdrive (with 'Kick down') also made its appearance.

72A Buick

72B Buick

72C Cadillac

72D Cadillac

72E Cadillac

72A: **Buick Eight Series 40 Special** Sport Coupé (with 'opera seats') Model 46S. This was Buick's cheapest offering, at $894. Wheelbase was 120 in., weight 3583 lb.
72B: **Buick Eight Series 60 Century** Touring Sedan with Trunk Back, Model 61. Again there were four Series: 40 Special, 60 Century, 80 Roadmaster, 90 Limited.
72C: **Cadillac Series 75 V8** Convertible Coupé had 141-in. wb. Other V8s: 61 with 126-in. and 60 with 127-in. wb. Series 90 was V16 in $5000 bracket.
72D: **Cadillac Series 60 V8** Sedan. Price in UK £850. This year Cadillac claimed: 'more than half of all fine (US) cars sold above $2000 are Cadillacs'.
72E: **Cadillac Series 75 V8** Fleetwood Limousine sold in Great Britain (with right-hand drive) at £1245 and had 5676-cc engine of 39·2 HP (RAC). Tyres 7·50 × 16.

Chevrolet 1939 came in two series, the **Master DeLuxe Series JA** and the **Master 85 Series JB,** both with 85-bhp 3·5-litre engine. The Master DeLuxe was the first Chevrolet with 'Knee Action' ifs with open (exposed) coil springs and was very popular. Vacuum-assisted steering column gear shift was optional at $20 extra. The Master 85 had a rigid front axle. Shown:
73A: Station Wagon with Midstates Body Corp. bodywork, available on JA and JB chassis ($883 and $848 respectively).
73B: Imperial seven-passenger model, produced by GM in Antwerp had 134-in. wb, divided prop shaft, ½-ton truck rear axle, 6·25 × 16 tyres.
73C: Period advertisement of Canadian-built Chevrolets. Prices: JA from £330, JB from £279.
73D: Sport Coupé, seating 2+2. Wheelbase of all models (except Imperial) was 112¼ in.
73E: Master DeLuxe Sport Sedan had built-in trunk.
73F: Master 85 Coupé with (removable) Pickup box.

73A Chevrolet

73B Chevrolet

73C Chevrolet

73D Chevrolet

73E Chevrolet

73F Chevrolet

74A: Chrysler Imperial. Part of a fleet of 260 fully equipped surgical units, mobile first-aid posts and ambulances supplied for use in Britain at the beginning of the war.

74B: Chrysler Imperial Eight had 5·3-litre L-head engine with 82·55 × 123·8 mm bore and stroke, wb 125 in. British Dodge D23 Custom Eight was virtually identical. Chrysler Custom Imperial had 144-in. wb.

74C: DeSoto offered DeLuxe SP7 and Custom S6 models with 114- and 119-in. wb respectively. Engine taxable HP ratings were 23·4 and 27·3 respectively. Shown is Custom S6 Sedan.

74D: Dodge D11 Luxury Liner Six had 117-in. wb and 217·8-cu in. 87-bhp engine. For export there were also the 114-in. wb D12 and D12X. HP ratings 25·3, 23·4 and 19·8 respectively.

74A Chrysler

74B Chrysler

74C DeSoto

74D Dodge

75A: **Ford V8 Model 91A DeLuxe 85 HP** Convertible Coupé (Body Type 76). Other body options included Tudor (70B), Fordor (73B) and Convertible Fordor (74) Sedans, Coupé (77B) and Station Wagon (79).

75B: **Ford V8 Model 91A Standard 85 HP** and **Model 922A 60 HP** had same sheet metal as 1938 DeLuxe. Body styles included Sedans (70A, 73A), Coupé (77A), Sedan Delivery (78, shown), Wagon (78).

75C: **British Model 62 2·2-litre,** produced 1936—39 (early models with spare wheel on back), then continued as 3·6-litre with military pattern front end.

75D: **French Matford F81 3·6-litre (and F82 2·2-litre),** 1938—39. Preceding F72 and F76 looked like British 62 but had built-in head-lamps and forward-opening front doors. 1946—48 2·2-litre Ford F472A was like F72 again but with divided windshield, heavier bumpers and column gearshift. 1937—40 Chenard et Walcker U17 also used the 3·6-litre V8.

75E: **German Ford V8 3·6-litre,** 1938—39. Also in production was Model 92 with 2·2-litre engine. Various American types were produced in Cologne from about 1931.

75A Ford

75B Ford

75C Ford (GB)

75D Ford (F)

75E Ford (D)

76A: Hudson One-Twelve Six Touring Brougham. This 112-in. wb series (various body options) was priced to compete with 'Big Three' offerings. Larger Hudsons had built-in headlamps.
76B: La Salle Series 50 V8 Two-passenger Coupé was Cadillac's least expensive model. It had a 120-in. wb. The make was discontinued in 1940.
76C: Lincoln Continental Convertible and Coupé were first built in 1939 (as 1940 model) under the direction of the late Edsel Ford. Similar models were made in 1940—41 and 1946—48.
76D: Lincoln Zephyr 96H V12 Sedan. 1939 models featured some styling changes including a new radiator grille with vertical bars, new bumpers, and other refinements.
76E: Mercury 99 V8 was introduced by Ford in 1938 for the 1939 model year. This new make was aimed at the medium price field.

76C Lincoln

76A Hudson

76D Lincoln

76B LaSalle

76E Mercury

page 77

77A: **Nash Ambassador Six** Model 3925 Coupé, seating three, was built on a 121-in. wb chassis. **Ambassador Eight** had 125-in. wb, and same six body styles. Low-priced **LaFayette** models (10 body styles) had similar appearance but were less luxurious, on 117-in. wb.

77B: **Oldsmobile** 1939 models had 'Rhythmic Ride', an all-coil spring suspension combined with 4-way stabilisation and 'Knee Action' ifs, 'Observation type' bodies by Fisher (similar to Chevrolet and Pontiac) and 'Handi-Shift' steering column gear control. Shown is rhd Sedan.

77C: **Oldsmobile F39 Sixty** was new introduction in the low-price field. Other series: Seventy and Eighty. By late March over 100,000 1939 models had been produced (more than total 1938 model production). For 1940 models Hydra-Matic was first offered as optional extra.

77A Nash

77B Oldsmobile

77C Oldsmobile

78A: **Packard Super Eight, Seventeenth Series, Model 1703** Four-door Touring Sedan (Body Type 1272) was offered at $1732 on 127-in. wb. Model 1705 had 148-in. wb.

78B: **Packard** Station Wagon with non-standard bodywork and some modifications to the lighting equipment, photographed in Spain. Cheapest 1939 model was Six (1700), priced from $888.

78C: **Plymouth** shared bodywork with other Chrysler Corp. products but all had distinguishing grilles and trim. Plymouth came in two series: P7 Roadking and P8 DeLuxe. In Britain the P8 was marketed as Chrysler Wimbledon Six (or P8X Kew Six with small-bore engine).

78B Packard

78C Plymouth

78A Packard

79A: Pontiac DeLuxe 115 Six, also known as 'Quality Six', had 115-in. wb. DeLuxe 120 Six and DeLuxe Eight had 120-in. wb. Six engine was 222·7-cu in., Eight 248·9-cu in., both L-head.

79B: Studebaker Champion Six was introduced in the spring as a new economical compact car. Custom and DeLuxe models were available with Coupé, Club Sedan (shown) and Cruising Sedan body styles.

79C: Studebaker State President Eight Club Sedan, like State Commander Six and Champion, was styled by Raymond Loewy. All models had independent front suspension with transversal leaf spring.

79D: Willys-Overland sold over 25,000 of its four-cylinder compact cars this year. In the annual Gilmore-Yosemite Economy Run they came first and second with over 26 mpg (US).

79A Pontiac

79C Studebaker

79B Studebaker

79D Willys

ABBREVIATIONS

AMA	Automobile Manufacturers Association, Inc.
B×S	bore and stroke
bhp	brake horsepower
cc	cubic centimetre (=0·061 cu in.)
CKD	completely knocked down
CR	compression ratio
cu in.	cubic inch (=16·39 cc)
HP	horsepower, NACC, SAE and RAC; in Britain also known as treasury rating or taxable horse-power
ifs	independent front suspension
in.	inch (=2·54 cm)
L-head	engine with side valves
NACC	National Automobile Chamber of Commerce, Inc.
ohv	overhead valves (I-head)
qv	*quod vide* (which see)
RAC	Royal Automobile Club (GB)
SAE	Society of Automotive Engineers
sv	side valves (L-head)
wb	wheelbase

SUMMARY OF MAJOR AMERICAN CAR MAKES
1930–39 (WITH DATES OF THEIR EXISTENCE)

CHRYSLER GROUP

Chrysler	(from 1923)
DeSoto	(1928–60)
Dodge	(from 1914)
Plymouth	(from 1928)

FORD GROUP

Ford	(from 1903)
Lincoln	(from 1920)
Mercury	(from 1938)

GENERAL MOTORS GROUP

Buick	(from 1903)
Cadillac	(from 1903)
Chevrolet	(from 1911)
LaSalle	(1927–40)
Marquette	(1929–31)
Oakland	(1907–31)
Oldsmobile	(from 1896)
Pontiac	(from 1926)
Viking	(1929–30)

OTHER MAKES

American Austin/Bantam	(1930–41)
Auburn	(1900–37)
Continental	(1933–34)
Cord	(1929–37)
Crosley	(1939–52)
DeVaux	(1931–32)
Duesenberg	(1920–37)
Durant	(1921–32)
Erskine	(1926–30)
Essex	(1918–32)
Franklin	(1901–34)
Graham (-Paige)	(1927–41)
Hudson	(1909–57)
Hupmobile	(1908–41)
LaFayette	(1934–39)
Marmon	(1902–33)
Nash	(1917–57)
Packard	(1899–1958)
Pierce-Arrow	(1901–38)
Reo	(1904–36)
Rockne	(1931–33)
Studebaker	(1902–66)
Stutz	(1911–35)
Terraplane	(1932–37)
Willys (-Overland)	(1908–63)

ACKNOWLEDGEMENTS

This book was compiled and written largely from historic source material in the library of the Olyslager Organisation and in addition photographs and/or other material was kindly provided or loaned by the following:

American Motors Corporation, Chrysler Corporation, Ford Motor Company (USA, Great Britain and Germany), General Motors Corporation, General Motors Limited, Kaiser Jeep Corporation, *Old Motor,* and the Pre-50 American Auto Club, as well as the private collections of Jan Bakker, G. A. Ingram, Clifford Lake, Fred van Leeuwen, Jan Polman and Bart H. Vanderveen. Thanks are also extended to Gerard W. Hitman and David J. Voller for valuable contributions and editorial comments.